40 QUESTIONS AND ANSWERS ON RELIGION

40 Questions and Answers On Religion

JACK FINEGAN

Based upon the author's full
length Haddam House book,
Youth Asks About Religion.

ASSOCIATION PRESS • *New York*

40 QUESTIONS AND ANSWERS ON RELIGION

Copyright ©️ 1958 by
National Board of Young Men's Christian Associations

Association Press, 291 Broadway, New York 7, N. Y.

Price, 50 cents

Library of Congress catalog card number: 58-6475

Printed in the United States of America

CONTENTS

I. God

III. THE BIBLE

IV. THE CHURCH

V. Immortality

40 QUESTIONS AND ANSWERS
ON RELIGION

I

GOD

1. Is It Intellectually Respectable to Believe in God?

IT SEEMS to be statistically respectable to believe in God. A Gallup poll, conducted in eleven nations, gave figures for belief in God ranging from sixty-six per cent of the population in France to ninety-six per cent in Brazil. In the United States, so the poll reported, ninety-four per cent of the people expressed a belief in the Deity.*

Probably it is also historically respectable to believe in God. Many of the greatest philosophers from Plato to' Kant to Whitehead have devoted much of their thought to God. Many of the greatest scientists, likewise, have been firm believers in God. The names of men like Tycho Brahe, Francis

* Documentation by chapters appears at the end of the book, begining on page 126. A briefly annotated list of Suggested Readings, two books for each chapter, is found on page 127.

Bacon, and Isaac Newton come immediately to mind. Furthermore, as Robert A. Millikan recorded with statistical documentation in his book, *Time, Matter and Values*,[1] among the "distinguished scientists" of today, more of the younger than of the older men report themselves to be believers in God. But none of us can decide a matter like this on the basis of statistics alone, or just by being told what certain other people think about it. We must ask for ourselves whether belief in God squares with our best possible understanding of the universe. Although we do it with far less certainty than twenty-five years ago, we may still give an affirmative answer. As we explore the universe and seek to understand evolution and history, the patternfulness of the world and the purposiveness of evolution still challenge us. It makes little intellectual sense to reduce all this to "chance." So little, indeed, does that make sense that even some who try to speak with complete scientific objectivity and impartiality have been driven to invent the term "antichance" to explain this great tendency which works through all things. If it is intellectually respectable to believe in "anti-chance" then certainly it is not less so to believe in God as the Creator of this orderly world and the Establisher of those purposes which drive toward far-off spiritual goals.

We must admit, however, the presence in the world of that which makes nature a test as well as a support of faith. This recognition underlines the fact that our belief in God ultimately rests less on our observations and discoveries than on his historical manifestations of himself to us. The Bible speaks of this God as a living Person who is engaged in active dealings with mankind. The God of the Bible is not an object to be found at the end of a long intellectual search but the Subject who himself takes the initiative in every relationship with his creatures. Man could never by his own wisdom find out this God if God himself had not first of all communicated himself to those he had made. Thus at last the question is not one of respectability, what others believe, or whether man can persuade himself to believe in an idea of God which he has constructed out of his own thinking. The issue is really whether man is willing to surrender his own presumptions and acknowledge the One who is approaching him at every turn and to whom he himself is object, creature, and child. Study of the world confirms rather than convinces us of the active presence of God in whom we find ourselves constrained to believe.

2. Is God Anthropomorphic?

Anthropomorphic is an English word made out of two Greek roots. The first, *anthropos*, was the Greek word for man, and it appears also in such modern terms as anthropology. The second Greek root is *morphe*, meaning form, which also occurs in an English word like morphology. Anthropomorphic means, therefore, in form like a man, and particularly refers to the representation or conception of God as being in human shape and with human attributes and emotions.

There is no doubt that in the third and eleventh chapters of Genesis, for example, whether they are intended literally or poetically, the representation of God is in anthropomorphic terms. In the first case, we have the story of the Garden of Eden and are told that the Lord God was "walking in the garden in the cool of the day." In the second case, we have the story of the Tower of Babel and are told that the Lord "came down to see the city and the tower, which the sons of men had built."

Now let us suppose that we want to avoid anthropomorphism. What shall we do? As Professor Streeter once pointed out, what modern man most often does is to fall into "mechanomorphism." Obsessed with his clever machines and impressed by the mechanical aspects of the universe, he thinks of God in mechanical terms. He envisions the universe as a vast machine and conceives total reality as existing in the form of a machine. Others who would no longer use the machine analogy so crudely still think of God in terms of impersonal law and process.

But this will hardly do! Here we are, personal individuals contemplating God and reducing him to something less than ourselves. Personality is self-conscious and purposive. These attributes apply neither to a machine nor to a law. Therefore, on the foregoing hypothesis, we are reduced to the absurdity of maintaining that a mechanistic, impersonal process has eventuated in the emergence of self-conscious, purposive personality.

It seems better, therefore, to take the position that personality is not only the highest fact within the

realm of our experience, but also the best clue to
the nature of ultimate reality. Since persons exist
and are able to think, experience beauty, and strive
after the right, there must be at the heart of the
universe a personal reality whose values are likewise those of truth, beauty, and goodness. This can
be called anthropomorphism if one will, but it is
assuredly a spiritual anthropomorphism. Indeed, it
must be said that anthropomorphism has commonly
been a mark of vitality in religion. A spiritual anthropomorphism which conceives the highest
reaches of man's life as having an essential kinship
with what is deepest in the nature of the universe
is not only a vital but also a logically defensible
position. It accords with the profound biblical insight which declares that "God created man in his
own image, in the image of God he created him."

The mere fact of human personality, however,
hardly convinces us of God's personal character, for
often our dominant impression of persons is of their
meanness, dissipation, twistedness, and unfaithful-
ness. Our ultimate conviction of the personal character of God rests rather on his disclosure of himself to us as a person. It is such meeting between
God and man, a highly personal confrontation, to

which the Bible bears witness. Man finds himself
in the presence of his Maker. His proper manner
of speech is not "I and It," but "I and Thou."
"Thou art . . ."; "Thou hast done . . ."; "Wilt
thou. . . ?" are the ways he addresses the One upon
whom his existence depends. Man becomes vividly
aware of his own creaturehood.

But God's divine self-disclosure also reveals the
sordidness of our lives, the need of human personality for redemption. Man realizes that he is dis-
obedient and that by simply redoubling his own
efforts he cannot hope to make himself acceptable
in the presence of the holy God. Indeed, the man
in the Bible who stands and boasts in his prayer of
his own self-achieved goodness is the very one most
clearly revealed as having failed to comprehend the
nature of the goodness of God. But the other man
who asks for the mercy of God because he knows
himself to be so unacceptable before Him is shown
to be the very one who is accepted. Thus the Bible
confirms our judgment that human personality itself
is the very area where God's redemption is needed.

God's self-giving in order to heal man's personality underlines his love for man and his suffering
with man. Love and suffering are pre-eminently

personal relations. It is on this basis of his self-disclosure, that we affirm that God is personal.

3. Is God the Sum Total of Human Ideals?

In the preceding section we saw how the Bible
states that God created man in his own image. In
modern times it has become fashionable among some
thinkers to declare that exactly the reverse is true,
that actually man created God in his own image.
The line of reasoning here employed suggests that
God is obviously an idea cherished by the human
mind. Man conceives the thought that there is a
Supreme Being and naturally pictures this Supreme
Being as like himself. Indeed, a rationalistic explanation of the idea of God somewhat of this sort
was given as long ago as the sixth century B.C.
when Xenophanes declared that if oxen, lions, and
horses were to carve images, they would fashion
gods after their own shapes and make them bodies
like their own. The highest form of this kind of
explanation appears in our day in the humanistic
affirmation that God is only the sum total of human
ideals. Man takes his highest hopes and purposes

and projects them against a cosmic background.
That is his God. The sooner we recognize that
God is not really there, and adjust ourselves to
working toward our own otherwise unsupported
ideals, the sooner we shall understand what life is
really like in this universe. Such is the argument.

What is wrong with that? One thing certainly
is wrong with it, namely, that it changes God from
an objective into a subjective reality, in the sense
of a reality which exists only in our own minds.
Now there is no need to deny that God is subjec-
tively apprehended by us. That simply means that
the only way we can know him is in our minds
and through ideas and experiences that are a part
of our own human life. But this is far from saying
that God has no existence save as an idea and an
ideal in our minds. It has been characteristic of
every great religion to believe that God is an objective reality. If there is any being whose existence
is derived and illusory, it is man himself. According
to Hinduism, man is caught in a net of illusion and
can escape only by recognizing the essential identity
of his soul with the Soul of the universe. In the Old
Testament, God is described as "from everlasting to
everlasting," and man as being "like grass which

is renewed in the morning: in the morning it
flourishes and is renewed; in the evening it fades
and withers." Surely, the very heart is taken out of
real religion if its central faith is destroyed, namely
that man is a created, dependent being, whose
Maker and Sustainer is One infinitely greater than
himself. Similarly, many lines of scientific and
philosophical reasoning converge toward the conclusion that the universe is only intelligible as the
result of a great purpose.

The God who reveals himself to Christian believers is One who at once shatters their natural,
prideful ideals and bodies forth for them radically
new and demanding ones. Man, in relating himself
to these divine imperatives, is not vainly endeavoring to lift himself up by his own bootstraps, but is
seeking to acknowledge his conscious dependence
on that mighty force not himself which makes for
righteousness. In the language of the Christian
faith, he has received the spirit of adoption whereby
he is enabled to call upon God as Father. This
active, intrusive God is Loving Claimant rather than
a human projection.

4. *What Is Your Definition of God?*

There is a bewildering variety of definitions of
God. Some are skeptical, and declare that he is the
Unknowable (Herbert Spencer), or explain that
he is an Illusion, born of the need to make tolerable
the helplessness of man and built out of the material
offered by memories of the helplessness of his own
childhood and the childhood of the race (Sigmund
Freud). Some are humanistic, and call him the
Common Will of Humanity (H. A. Overstreet),
the Symbol of the Highest Social Values (E. S.
Ames), or the Imagined Synthesis of Ideal Ends
(John Dewey). Some are naturalistic, and identify
him as the Principle of Concretion (A. N. Whitehead), or as that Order of Existence and Possibility
by virtue of which the greatest possible good is truly
a possibility and can be achieved by human effort
(H. N. Wieman). Some are descriptive of an
emerging deity, and say that he is a Growing God
(William James), or the Spiritual Nisus of an
evolving universe (C. L. Morgan). Some picture
him as finite, and state that he is a conscious Person

of Perfect Good Will limited by the free choices of
other persons and by restrictions within his own
nature (E. S. Brightman), or an Eternal Cosmic
Mind who suffers when matter makes his plans
miscarry (J. E. Boodin). Some use the analogy of
a particular aspect of man's mental processes and
call God the Cosmic Mathematician (Sir James
Jeans), and others decline to use any human comparison whatsoever, and call God the Utterly Other
(Karl Barth). A biblical definition, found in John
4:24, is the concise statement, "God is spirit." In
the common usage of the word, "spirit" is that
which is capable of living, thinking, willing, and
loving. Thus God is a personal Being who lives,
thinks, wills, and loves, and who is the universal
source of life, thought, righteous purpose, and noble
love. Having created the universe and man, he
sustains and redeems them.

In philosophical thought about religion it seems
necessary to try to define God. Yet, having formulated the best definition of which our minds are
capable, we are reminded of the French saying,
Dieu défini est Dieu fini. With a play on words
that can hardly be reproduced in English, this
sentence declares that God defined is God finished.

The infinite greatness of God cannot be brought within the compass of a small definition; if it be so confined it is lost. Hence, beyond all our definitions we would retain a sense of wonder and amazement in the presence of him who so utterly exceeds the bounds of our comprehension.

5. What Varieties of Belief in God Are There?

There are, as this question suggests, many varieties of belief in God. In order to describe and classify them, a series of technical terms has been devised. The basic root in the formation of these terms is derived from the Greek word *theos*, meaning God. To the root is added the suffix *-ism*, signifying belief or doctrine. Thus *theism*, etymologically, connotes belief in God in general. To this word, various prefixes are joined to specify particular kinds of faith. The first prefix is the letter a-, which serves as a sort of minus sign, and gives the word *atheism*, meaning belief that there is no God. Next comes *polytheism*, which means belief in many gods. Since there are many forces at work in nature man early conceived the existence of numerous deities to account for these manifestations. Such belief in a multiplicity of divine beings has continued to characterize many living religions. *Kathenotheism* is the tendency within polytheism to give the supreme place to one god for a time, and then to another, one after the other. *Henotheism* is belief in one god, though not to the theoretical exclusion of the existence of others. *Monotheism* is belief in only one God. It is often customary to use the word *theism* to connote belief in one personal God. *Panentheism* is the doctrine that God includes the world as a part of his being, but is not the whole of it. *Theopantheism* is the teaching that God is all, and *pantheism* the almost indistinguishable doctrine that all is God. Such are the ranges of thought about God, from the denial of his existence at one extreme to the affirmation at the other extreme, that all that there is is God. Towering up between is the central faith in one supreme personal being, Creator of the world but not identical with it, who is God.

Since discussion often proceeds with terms which are philosophical rather than strictly theological, three other technical words should also be mentioned. These are: *pluralism*, the theory that there are many different principles at work in the universe; *dualism*, the belief that the universe is divided between two mutually opposed elements; and *monism*, the doctrine that there is only one kind of ultimate reality.

6. Is God Interested in Human Individuals?

In space and time man is almost utterly insignificant. In a universe the dimensions of which are measured in millions of light-years, the earth is a hardly noticeable speck of dust. Yet this is the only home man has. Furthermore, it is but a small part of the total surface of this speck of dust that is actually occupied by man. The whole human race could be put into a cubical box one mile on each side, and this could be swallowed up by that single crack in the earth's surface which we call the Grand Canyon. If the total two billion inhabitants of the earth constitute a no more impressive mass than this, how diminutive must any single individual seem.

Similarly, when measured against universal time, the existence of man seems extremely brief. Speaking of the earth alone, its total age may be two billion years. The modern genus of man first appeared about 100,000 years ago. That makes the whole life of the human race occupy only the last 1/20,000th part of the age of the earth. As for the Christian Era, it fills only the last one-millionth part of the earth's age. Again, if we think of the life span of an individual man, it is a yet more infinitesimal fraction of cosmic time.

Such figures as these often produce what someone has called "astronomical intimidation." There is perhaps no better reply than the other remark that "astronomically speaking, man is the astronomer." If we were to ask for one of the largest things in the universe, we might think of the star Betelgeuse, which has a diameter three hundred times that of our sun. But what is it? An enormous mass of incandescent gas which man measures. As an illustration of a long enduring thing, we might recall a great redwood tree that has had a living existence of over two thousand years. But it knows not itself, and it is man who brings to it an awareness that combines scientific calculation concerning it with esthetic appreciation of its majesty and beauty.

In what would God be interested in all his vast universe? Only in things which have large size or which last a long time? Will he not be concerned with those beings which, apparently tiny and transitory as they are, are endowed with "godlike" gifts of self-awareness, thought, and appreciation?

Although the Bible was written prior to the period of modern scientific discovery, it reveals a keen sense of the relative insignificance and the ephemeral quality of man's life. The insignificance of man is described in the eighth Psalm:

> When I look at thy heavens, the work of thy fingers,
> the moon and the stars which thou hast established;
> what is man that thou art mindful of him,
> and the son of man that thou dost care for him?[2]

But the Bible also gives us precisely the insight for which we have been striving. The eighth Psalm continues immediately:

> Yet thou hast made him little less than God,
> and dost crown him with glory and honor.

This is the dignity of man. He is endowed with attributes which are related to those of God himself.

But the Christian faith that God is concerned about man, every single human individual, rests

not only upon the initial act of God in the creation
of man but also upon the many acts, attested in the
Bible, in which God has visited man and sought
him out for his own salvation. Of all these acts the
chief is that in which God has sent Jesus Christ to
seek and to save the lost. As we see in the Gospels
the love of Jesus for every last, least, and lost child
of God, it is brought home to us that God, indeed,
knows and cares for each one of us. God has thus
manifested the depth of his love and concern for
us in the life of Jesus Christ.

7. How Can One Believe in God When There Is So Much Evil in the World?

This is perhaps the oldest and most stubborn
problem of all and it may even be insoluble from
our limited point of view. Nevertheless, it seems
necessary to seek at least the best answer we can to
the question. This has been sought along the lines
both of reason and of faith.

Intellectual considerations direct attention to the
following facts: First, a great deal of what seems
evil to us is simply the work of an orderly universe.

The behavior of the universe, as described by the laws of science, is faithful and regular. The law of gravity is not suspended in order to save a man from harm when he falls off a roof. It may be that the *man* is disorderly! The suspension might cause an amount of damage to other persons far out-weighing the benefit to this man. Furthermore, we would never really learn to be "orderly" about falls if the law of gravity were constantly being nullified in emergencies. The existence of law in the uni-verse sometimes seems to work for our harm, but it could not really be otherwise if we are to learn to live.

In the second place, a great deal of evil certainly comes because man has the power of free choice. In exercising his power of freedom, he often chooses what is wrong. These wrong choices bring disaster and suffering.

In the third place, man lives in a social solidarity. He is intimately interconnected with his fellows throughout the whole web of society. Indeed, in our day these interconnections ramify until they extend all around the world. Thus it is that the ignorant act or wrong deed of some person may have far-reaching effects. The consequences of the act may fall upon those who are utterly innocent.

These three facts seem at least partially to explain some of the evils in the world. Evils come because of our ignorance of the laws of the universe and of life, because of our perverse and sinful choices in the face of the great alternatives of right and wrong, and because of the interconnectedness of society which allows the baleful effects of wrongdoing to spread out over ever-widening circles and down through successive generations. These very same conditions that open the way for evil also open the way for all learning, moral development, and human progress. If we did not confront a partially ordered universe we could never develop any reliable understanding of life. If we did not face genuine alternatives of right and wrong, we could never grow in moral stature. If we did not live together in a society, we could not share the benefits of the insights and achievements of others.

However, beyond these evils for which partial explanation can be given lies that area of the demonic: wild, natural catastrophes like avalanches and tidal waves; baffling mental and physical malformations, for which there is no simple explanation. If not willed directly by God (as surely these calamities are not), and not directly attributable to man, then this body of evil must be the result of waywardness in the world itself, cosmic freedom gone astray. Our problem is not so much that of the origin of these demonic forces, as one of ascertaining whether there really exists a power able to conquer evil in this realm, at its deepest levels. Has God, in permitting these hideous events to transpire, abandoned us to a universe part iron-clad, part fortuitous?

Manifestly not! God enters the arena of human history and suffers with man to bring triumph out of seeming defeat. God is the Lord even over death, sin, and chance. His overlordship brings life out of tragedy, meaning out of chaos, love out of bitterness. Though he may seem to lose some battles, God never loses the War. Therefore, evil, black and terrible as it is, need not drive us to the doubt and denial of God. It is evident that we live in the kind of world where it is possible and necessary to *combat* evil, and we may believe that God desires to help us to do so.

It is not likely that a thoughtful person who has seen or felt pain will be finally satisfied by any intellectual explanation of its place in the world.

In the midst of severe personal suffering—his own or someone else's—he cannot stop to "reason" it out. Then it is that he needs *faith* that "underneath are the everlasting arms." In the presence of pain and humiliation and defeat one can still feel himself sustained by Another, who comforts him, and strengthens him to put forth every ounce of energy to correct and change evil to good, believing that the effort is worth while. For in Jesus Christ he sees a God who knows the cost of evil, who bears its consequences, and who is—with his suffering—the Sovereign Lord of the universe.

8.   Can a Miracle Happen?

According to a materialist a miracle cannot take place. The universe operates according to its laws, and there can be no deviation from them. According to conservative religious belief, on the other hand, any kind of miracle can take place any time, if God wills it to. Which is correct?

The first view, which denies the possibility of any miracle, seems to imprison God within his universe. The second, which thinks miracles may occur

at any time, seems to disregard the very structure of
reality which we believe represents God's thought
and purpose. Therefore neither conception is very
satisfying to a thoughtful person. Is it possible to
look at the matter from any other point of view?

The following theory defines miracles in three
ways, and says frankly that the first kind of "miracle" probably never takes place, but that the other
two kinds do. The first type of miraculous happening would be an arbitrary interference with the
faithful regularity of the behavior of the universe.
It would be an act of God *contrary* to the laws of
his world. The temporary suspension of the law of
gravity would be a case in point. There is little
evidence that such a "miracle" ever takes place. As
far as we know, no authentic example of such an
event has been observed, and as far as we can see,
such an act on the part of God would be out of
harmony with his own nature.

The second type of miracle is a happening that
is wonderful to those concerned and quite beyond
their own power to accomplish, but it takes place
through the working of the regular known laws of
the universe. It is the working together of the
various factors involved, and their convergence

upon the particular time, place, and people, that is remarkable and beyond the reach of human power. Many of the miracles in the Bible would seem to fall within this category. If the crossing of the arm of the Red Sea by the children of Israel was made possible by the favorable and concurrent action of tide and wind, and if the falling of the walls of Jericho was due to an earthquake at the time the Israelites came there, then that people surely would thank God for wonderful deliverance and wonderful victory.

The third kind of miracle is an event in which God acts through laws *beyond* those now known to man. There is reason to believe that there are great reaches of the universe and its laws that still lie far beyond the ken of man. Possibly some of these laws may become better known as man grows in moral and spiritual character, as he progresses in stages of evolution that have as yet barely begun. But God can work through such higher reaches of reality even now, perhaps in answer to the prayers by which men of faith touch realms beyond rational comprehension. The miracles of healing performed by Christ may illustrate the working of such higher laws, some of which are now coming dimly into view in the understanding of man as a "psychosomatic" being whose mind and body intimately affect each other.

That God should actually work in the ways supposed by our second and third types of miracles, to answer prayer and to bring good into human life beyond what man can do, is in harmony both with his own nature and with the essential structure of his universe. That God actually has wrought wondrously in his dealings with man we are assured in the Bible. Indeed, it is in what Jesus Christ has revealed to us of the nature of God as a caring, concerned, solicitous Father that we find the criterion by which to decide about miracle. About any so-called miraculous occurrence must we not in the last analysis ask the following question? "Does this agree with or distort and conflict with that understanding of God which we have of him as the Father of Jesus Christ?"

II

JESUS CHRIST

9. *Did Jesus Really Live?*

THROUGH THE comparative study of religions it has become well known that myth and legend play a part in many faiths. The Mystery Religions, for example, which prevailed widely in the Roman Empire in the first century A.D., were often based upon the mythical experiences of some god or goddess. Osiris, Isis, Horus, Cybele, Demeter, and Mithras, were some of the deities around whom such cults were centered. Was Christianity just another such Mystery Religion with an equally mythical founder? Lewis Browne gives the answer in his book, *This Believing World*,[1] when he is endeavoring to explain why it was that Christianity won the victory in a world that was already so full of other faiths. "Only the Christians," he remarks, "had a real man to worship."

Do we have dependable knowledge of Jesus as an actual historical person? Yes. In the first place we have the testimony of the letters of Paul. This testimony is particularly significant, for two reasons: One is that this man was at first an enemy of Christianity. He would hardly have been persuaded to join this movement if he had known that its founder had never existed, but was only a myth manufactured in men's imaginations. Another reason for giving special importance to what we learn of the historical Jesus in Paul's letters, is the simple fact that this information is so very incidental and casual. The letters were written for the purpose of helping churches and individuals with specific problems and questions. But they indirectly disclose a great many facts about Jesus' life and his character and work. Paul and the other Christians knew them perfectly well, from unimpeachable witnesses, and simply took them for granted.

In the second place we have the evidence of the Synoptic Gospels. These are the first three Gospels, called "synoptic" because they all look at the life of Jesus from the same point of view. As careful, comparative scrutiny discloses, the oldest sources here are the Gospel according to Mark, and a Collection of the Sayings of Jesus, now lost in its original form, but utilized by Matthew and Luke. From the Synoptic Gospels we are enabled to see the life of Jesus in a comprehensive historical context, and to feel the impact of his personality and message.

In the third place we have the witness of the other documents of the New Testament. Most or all of them are later than these we have already mentioned, but even though they are concerned with new problems in the life of the church, and reflect advancing thought, they contain much important information about Jesus, and clearly show forth the essential character of his life.

Now it is certainly true that all the various New Testament documents have to be studied historically and scientifically, but it may be affirmed confidently that they provide us with the strongest kind of evidence for the historical existence of Jesus. Indeed, another great Jewish scholar, Joseph Klausner, declares, "If we had ancient sources like those in the Gospels for the history of Alexander or Caesar, we should not cast any doubt upon them whatsoever."

10. What Facts Can We Be Sure of About His Life?

We cannot be sure of the exact date of the birth of Jesus. One would suppose this date was identical with the beginning of the Christian Era, but actually there was a certain amount of error in the calculation of the beginning point of this Era. The Gospels tell us that Jesus was born when Herod was King of the Jews, and we know from secular history that Herod died in 4 B.C. Therefore Jesus must have been born not later than in that year.

We know approximately how old Jesus was when he began his public work. Luke tells us this explicitly: "Jesus, when he began his ministry, was about thirty years of age."

And we know with a good degree of assurance, the date of the crucifixion of Jesus. All the Gospels tell us that this event took place on a Friday, and the Gospel according to John shows that Jesus was crucified at the same time that the Passover Lamb was slain by the Jews for their great annual religious feast. Combining these facts with laboriously calculated astronomical tables and calendars, Professor A. T. Olmstead, in his book, *Jesus in the Light of History*,[2] gives the exact date of the crucifixion as April 7, A.D. 30.

Now something like this same state of affairs prevails with regard to everything about the life of Jesus. The information is relatively scanty for the earlier years: it increases sharply for the period of his actual ministry, and it is fullest of all in regard to the Last Week and the death of Jesus. This is natural, for the early church was concerned most of all with what Jesus did and said in his actual work, and with how he laid down his life for his followers.

Concerning the dependability of our knowledge of these matters, Professor E. F. Scott has remarked, "We need to begin with the great indubitable facts —that Jesus inspired his followers with a boundless devotion, that he brought good tidings to the poor and distressed, that he worked for the kingdom of God and was faithful unto death. These are the foundations of the history, and no criticism can shake them."

11. Is "Christ" a Name or a Title?

Jesus is the name that was given to the founder of Christianity at his birth, as we are told in Matthew 1:21. This name was frequently used among the Jewish people. It is the same as the Old Testament name Joshua, or Jeshua. It has appeared recently on some stone ossuaries of the first century A.D., found in a cave-tomb between Jerusalem and Bethlehem. Here we find that one man, for example, was named Jesus Aloth.

In contrast with the personal name of Jesus, Christ was originally a title. It is the same word in Greek as the word "Messiah" in Hebrew. This word literally means "anointed." The significance of it goes all the way back to ancient times when the Hebrew king was installed in his royal office by the ceremony of anointing. Then, after their political nation was destroyed and they no longer had a king on the throne at Jerusalem, the Jewish people hoped very much that sometime in the future God would raise up a new king for them and restore their national glory. To this coming King and Deliverer, they naturally applied the title, the

"Anointed One," that is, the Messiah, or the Christ. Around this title, then, all their hopes and longings for a better future were gathered. Sometimes they anticipated that the Messiah would be a literal king, reigning with a mighty sword at Jerusalem and destroying all their enemies; again they supposed that he would be a heavenly Judge, who would pronounce doom upon all the ungodly; and again, as in the books of Zechariah and Isaiah, they thought that he would be one who was meek and lowly, and a suffering servant of mankind.

When Jesus once asked his followers, "Who do men say that I am?" they reported that the common opinion was that Jesus was John the Baptist come back to life again after being slain by Herod Antipas, or that he was Elijah whose return to earth was expected before the end of the world, or that he was some other one of the prophets. When Jesus asked, "But who do you say that I am?" Peter answered on behalf of the group, "You are the Christ." They believed he was not simply a prophet, or one of the forerunners of the kingdom of God, but none other than the long-hoped-for Messiah who would actually establish that kingdom.

This has been the faith of the followers of Jesus

ever since, and inasmuch as they are disciples of the
"Christ" they have become known as "Christ-ians."
This name was first applied to them in the city of
Antioch, as we are told in Acts 11:26.

Strictly speaking, then, Jesus was the personal
name, and Christ the title of the founder of Christianity. But appropriately and properly enough, men
came to refer to him generally by both these words
at the same time. Ere long it was almost forgotten
that "Christ" was anything but a part of a personal
name too. Hence we commonly speak of him as
Jesus Christ. Paul did this regularly, and sometimes also reversed the two names and said Christ
Jesus. It is perfectly proper to do this, but it en-
riches our understanding if we remember that using
the word "Christ" carries with it the very confession
of our faith in the one who was "anointed" by God
to establish his kingdom.

12. What Is the Kingdom Which Jesus Proclaimed?

According to Mark 1:15, the very first preaching
of Jesus was an announcement of the kingdom of

God. This kingdom was a Jewish hope. The children of Israel shared with other Semitic peoples the conception that God was their king. The other Semitic peoples did not get much further with the idea. They thought that the god of their tribe was their king. Therefore, if they were overcome in battle, their king was also defeated. The god of some other tribe was more powerful than their own. The Israelite people attained a loftier conception of God than that. They believed that there was only one God over all the nations, and that he ruled with righteousness. But this seemed to be contradicted by the hard facts of experience. Within their own nation not everyone was obedient to God, and outside among the heathen there was an arrogant flaunting of human pride against God. Thus, the Israelites believed the time was yet to come when God would manifest his power and establish his as yet unseen rule in visible reality. This strong anticipation enabled the Jewish people to endure exile and persecution with dauntless faith.

When Jesus came preaching the kingdom of God he proclaimed it as a tremendous, imminent reality which was even then making its demands upon man. In Jesus' understanding the coming of the kingdom involved repentance, searching ethical demands, and a trusting, filial response to God as Father. Pre-eminently the kingdom was marked by certain standards of perfection in terms of which the whole imperfect life of man is judged. It was a New Covenant. This was the reality which was pressing in upon men.

So stupendous is this reality that it is no wonder if it is described in paradoxical terms. Thus as Jesus told about the kingdom of God he spoke of it as something which belongs to the future but also as something which is even now present. In the prayer Jesus taught his disciples are the words: "Thy kingdom come, thy will be done, on earth as it is in heaven." Surely as long as war, slums, crime, drunkenness, race hatred, and starvation exist, the will of God is not yet fully done and the final, triumphant coming of his kingdom is earnestly and ardently to be hoped for and prayed for. Yet, on the other hand, the kingdom is in a real sense already present. It is here now in the ceaseless activity of God, and it is present in the mighty deeds of Jesus. "The kingdom of God is in the midst of you," Jesus told his disciples, and to his antagonists he declared, "If it is by the finger of God that I cast

out demons, then the kingdom of God has come
upon you."

Similarly, the kingdom of God is both something
outward and something inward. When it comes it
will involve such a rearrangement of society that
the abuses which disfigure the present will be
eliminated and those perfections of which we dream
will be visibly manifest. But we ourselves cannot
live a hundred years, or a thousand years, or a mil-
lion years, waiting for the kingdom to come. Can
we then have none of it? Yes, according to the
teaching of Jesus, we can possess it inwardly even
now. "The kingdom of God," he declared, according to the alternative translation of Luke 17:21, "is
within you." Paul, the great follower and inter-
preter of Jesus, wrote, "The kingdom of God does
not mean food and drink but righteousness and
peace and joy in the Holy Spirit."

Once again, the kingdom of God is something
very great but also something very simple. Of course
it is a great thing because it involves God's rule of
this stupendous universe, and the ultimate perfect
establishment of his holy will. But the kingdom is
also something very simple and close at hand. The
Reverend H. R. L. Sheppard has told the story of

a great artist who in his old age said that he could remember perfectly the first occasion when he deliberately turned his back on the kingdom of God. He was a schoolboy at the time, home for the holidays and, as he walked down the village street, a small girl to whom he was something of a hero ran out of a cottage and offered him a bunch of rather faded flowers, doubtless the very best she could procure. The boy passed her by without taking the gift. Later, a little ashamed, he looked back and saw the child in tears and the flowers scattered on the road. Dr. Sheppard said: "I believe the offer of the Kingdom is the invitation which Jesus daily gives to you and to me to permit love and not hate to prevail now and here in our life, our work, and our home."

God here and now calls men into a new relationship to himself and others, into a covenanted community which serves as a leaven in the loaf of society, into a kingdom which is and is not fully yet.

13. What Did Jesus Christ Wish to Accomplish?

Since Jesus accepted the confession of his disciples that he was the Christ, he must have wished to establish the kingdom of God. As we have seen, this kingdom was the first thing of which he spoke as he began his public preaching. Now many people thought that the only way the kingdom of God could be established was by the rise of a military Messiah who would drive the hated Roman oppressors out of the land and re-establish the anciently splendid kingdom of the Jews. Such a kingdom might even be extended to encompass many heathen lands, some of the nationalistic prophets believed. There is good reason for supposing that when the devil showed Jesus all the kingdoms of the world in a moment of time, and offered to give them all to him, it was really a temptation to pursue the militaristic way of conquest and seek the goal of national glory. Jesus refused this way.

Other popular opinion at the time anticipated that the kingdom of God would be established by

supernatural intervention. Remembering the vi-
sions in the book of Daniel, not a few people
looked toward the clouds of heaven and expected
to see the Messiah someday seated there, conduct-
ing the Last Judgment. The devil also, we remember, suggested to Jesus that he perform supernatural
wonders such as casting himself down from the
pinnacle of the Temple and having the angels bear
him up; and his own disciples are reported in Luke
19:11 to have "supposed that the kingdom of God
was to appear immediately," evidently in some such
supernatural fashion as corresponded with the popular expectation. But Jesus did nct do anything
like this.

What then did he wish to accomplish? He
wished to establish the kingdom of God, not in the
way which corresponded to the superficial anticipa-
tions of the multitude, but in the way which ful-
filled the will of God himself. This is the reply
he made to the insidious temptations of Satan,
when he quoted Deuteronomy 6:13, "You shall
worship the Lord your God and him only shall you
serve." Therefore he followed the guidance of the
Spirit of God in his heart, and walked along a way
that led to the Cross, and to the imperishable estab-

lishment of a spiritual kingdom in the hearts of men.

The very fact that Jesus had to go to the Cross in the fulfillment of his work on behalf of the kingdom of God shows that that kingdom though desired by men was also resisted by men. In bodying forth the kingdom of God, in proclaiming God's reign, Jesus also seems bent on disclosing the true nature of man as estranged from God by sin and incapable of entering the kingdom without a radical change within himself. Thus Jesus not only reveals the character of God and of the coming kingdom, but also through his words and deeds brings to light the true nature of man. He seems intent on healing, on making whole; on forgiving, on making it possible for us to forgive ourselves; on teaching, on illuminating existence; and on empowering men to live new lives. Thus supremely Jesus wished to accomplish the reconciliation of the world unto God.

14. What Did He Teach?

Instead of founding a military empire or performing supernatural exploits, Jesus Christ "went

about . . . teaching (Matthew 4:23). From one of
his own parables we can see how this was an integral and indispensable part of establishing God's
kingdom. The parable was the story of the sower
who went out to sow. Some of his seed fell on the
path and was trodden under foot; some fell on
rocky ground and soon withered; some fell among
thorns and was choked; some "fell into good soil
and brought forth grain . . . yielding . . . a hun-
dredfold." Though Jesus may have simply left this
parable as it stood and expected his disciples to
comprehend its meaning, the Gospels contain an
explicit explanation of it as a setting forth of the
secrets of the kingdom of God. The seed is the
word of God, planted by Jesus in the field of the
world, some of which, received in faithful lives,
will grow into the fruits of the kingdom.

What sort of teachings, then, did Jesus give as
the creative principles of the kingdom of God?
There are many rich and varied things which he
said, all of them in their impact being nothing less
than tremendous, "gigantesque" words, as E. C.
Colwell has said in *An Approach to the Teaching
of Jesus*.[3] But when they asked him for the most
important truth of all, he responded with a two-

fold teaching: "The first is . . . 'You shall love the
Lord your God . . .' The second is . . . 'You shall
love your neighbor as yourself.'" The teaching of
Jesus is therefore in the first instance a profoundly
religious teaching. It relates the life of man to the
ultimate ground of his existence, and calls upon
him to love God completely. In the second instance, and intimately related to the first, it is a
dynamically ethical and social teaching. It calls for
love of one's fellow man, without any of the limits
which were customarily associated with such a
teaching in the Old Testament.

The kind of love which Jesus called for is desig-
nated in the New Testament by the Greek word
agape. In the wonderfully precise Greek language
there are no less than three words which are all
customarily translated by "love" in English. One is
eros, from which our word "erotic" is derived; another is *philia*, which means friendship; and the
third is *agape*. Agape is the distinctive kind of
Christian love. Perhaps it is best to define it simply
as the kind of attitude and concern which Jesus
himself manifested. In relation to God, then, love
is an attitude of trust in the heavenly Father; in

relation to man, it is compassionate concern and intelligent good will.

The call for the exercise of this kind of love was grounded in the knowledge that such love belongs to the nature of God himself. The center of the teaching of Jesus was God—God known as the righteous and terrible Judge, yet infinitely merciful Father. Like the prophets before him whose teaching he continued and reinterpreted, Jesus underlines the inward, moral dimensions of God's demand rather than its outward, ceremonial aspects, and culminates his ethic with an uncompromising demand for perfection. Men must be perfect as their heavenly Father is perfect. In short, his is a humanly impossible teaching, one which stresses man's need for God and the hopeless confusion of life apart from him.

15.   Did Jesus Actually Heal People?

As complete a record as we have of a day in the ministry of Christ is that which is found in Mark 1:21-34. This day was spent in Capernaum, a prominent city of New Testament times on the western shore of the Sea of Galilee. This day was the Jewish Sabbath, and Mark's Gospel pictures Jesus going into the synagogue and teaching there. In the synagogue, however, was "a man with an unclean spirit," and Jesus made the unclean spirit come out of him. As far as we can tell, the unclean spirit represented a mental malady of some sort, and Jesus healed the man thus afflicted. The next thing we are told in the record of this same day is that Jesus went to the home of Simon and Andrew after leaving the synagogue. There he found that Simon's mother-in-law was sick with a fever, and he healed her of this. The report of these wonderful deeds evidently spread rapidly, for we read further that when evening came, that is, when the Jewish Sabbath was over, and free movement and work were possible, a large number of sick and afflicted people were brought to his door. Mark states, "And he healed many who were sick with various diseases, and cast out many demons."

What shall we do with accounts such as these? We may ignore them, because it is hard to give a scientific explanation of them, but that is not too satisfactory. We may endeavor to eliminate them

from the records of the life of Christ as stories
spun by wonder-loving imaginations. Perhaps some
of the stories have been so developed or heightened.
There are too many of them, however, throughout
all the Gospels, and they constitute too often an
integral part of the account, to make it possible for
us to tear them all out.

Again, we may try to rationalize them. This was
done by such early writers on the life of Christ as
Herder and Paulus, for example. The typical rationalistic explanation would run something like
this: Simon's mother-in-law, for example, had been
sick for some time and her fever had run its course.
When Jesus came to her home and took her hand
and lifted her up, this provided the little extra
stimulus to enable her to shake off her lassitude
and return to the normal course of life, a thing
which she would very shortly have done anyway.
This type of explanation, however, makes Jesus
virtually an impostor, since he apparently took advantage of such situations to heighten his own
fame. As Albert Schweitzer said about rationalism,
"The method is doomed to failure because the
author only saves his own sincerity at the expense
of that of his characters."

The only remaining alternative, then, seems to
be to accept the fact that Christ actually performed
what we call "miracles" of healing. The philosophical background for understanding such happenings
has already been laid in our answer to the question
whether miracles can happen. We have there reasoned that there may well be higher laws in the
universe other than those with which we are yet
familiar. One who is able to work in harmony with
those higher laws could accomplish results which
would seem nothing less than miraculous. There
seems to be a distinct possibility, then, that Jesus
was operating in a realm of the mind and spirit
where there are wonderful possibilities yet little
known and realized by man in general.

One illustration may make this more plain. It
may be found in the book, *After Everest*,[4] by T.
Howard Somervell. Somervell was a mountaineer
who participated in one of the early attempts to
climb Mount Everest. After the expedition was
over, he traveled in India and saw the unrelieved
suffering of that land. Being a doctor, he went
there to work as a medical missionary. To the
hospital where he was stationed came a man upon
whom a leg operation had been performed by an

unskilled surgeon. X rays revealed that the whole
bone of the leg was infected from top to bottom
with tubercular disease. When told that amputation
offered the only chance of saving his life, the man
replied unexpectedly, "Will you give me three
weeks? I want to try the effect of praying about
it." He left the hospital, ill and with a fever,
capable only of being carried about. Three weeks
later, true to his promise, he returned, this time
hobbling with a stick and looking much better. The
X ray showed that the leg was improved, though
not yet free from the disease. Three weeks later he
came back again, and at that time the leg was
found to be healed. A few months later and he was
back at his regular work as a teacher in a boys'
mission school. The man explained simply that he
and his family and friends had joined in a chain
of prayer asking for healing. Somervell remarks,
"He and his family had proved that the age of
miracles is not over. Who can say what contribu-
tion India may not make to the religion of the
world when she has, like this man and his family,
been introduced to God as Christ showed Him?"

We must, however, also remember that so great
a saint and servant of Christ as the apostle Paul

earnestly besought release from a physical affliction and received not the material healing which he asked but rather the spiritual sustaining indicated by the words, "My grace is sufficient for you." We are not dealing therefore with the practice of magic but with the realm of faith.

God's ultimate will is always the flowering of the human spirit, but he has given men the abilities by which war with his will is sometimes carried on. It is this intermediate realm of genuine human freedom—where human agents may partially stifle and resist and fail fully to grasp the whole-making powers in the universe—which complicates discussion of divine healing. Human agents must be used by God in the realization of his purposes, but these agents may frustrate initially his plans, for they are often all too human and erring.

16. Why Did Jesus Die?

Many historical factors contributed to the death of Christ. The Roman imperial system constituted one of these. It was organized to preserve law and order. This meant, according to Roman ideas, the unhesitating liquidation of any revolutionaries who imperiled the existing order. The watch for such fomenters of rebellion was particularly sharp in Palestine because that land had been a veritable seed-plot of revolt. When Jesus, therefore, was accused to the Roman procurator as one who pretended to be a king, it became immediately probable that his life would be forfeited.

Another factor was the Jewish religious system. With all its noble aspects of spiritual insight and ethical imperative, this system had to a considerable extent hardened into a structure of legalism and ritualism. When, therefore, Jesus freely broke proscriptions relating to Sabbath observance and fearlessly drove out of the temple courts those who polluted it with commercialism, he was certain to become the object of bitter antagonism from those whose vested interests were bound up with the religious system as it stood.

The everlasting weaknesses of human nature also played their part in the chain of events which led to the death of Jesus. At one time, the multitudes of people were enthusiastic about him. Again, they were transformed into a mob crying for his death. Among Christ's own disciples, there was one who

betrayed him. Whether the traitorous deed of
Judas was done out of sheer avarice and disloyalty,
or perhaps with the thought of forcing Jesus at last
to declare himself as a supernatural king, we do
not know. Nevertheless, the deed was done and
it contributed its part to the tragic outcome.

It would be possible to enumerate yet other historical forces which converged toward the crucifixion of Christ, but all these factors together seem
insufficient to really explain the death of Jesus. He
does not impress us as one who simply died as the
unwilling victim of forces which were beyond his
control. Rather, one who had meditated profoundly
upon the deepest significance of the life of Christ
reported his saying about the laying down of his
life, "No one takes it from me, but I lay it down
of my own accord." That is certainly borne out by
the things which Jesus did. When he was warned
to flee from Galilee because Herod wanted to kill
him, he continued his work without the slightest
deviation on account of that threat. When he
started to Jerusalem and his own disciples urged
him not to go on account of the dangers there, he
nevertheless went steadfastly on. When he went
to the Garden of Gethsemane to pray, he was do-

ing, Luke tells us, exactly what his regular custom was. There was no slightest attempt to hide or flee. In brief, he took every step with wide-open eyes and clearly formed purpose.

Why then did he die? Because man refused to die to himself. Because in the will and way of God, this was necessary for the accomplishment of his work. Long before, a prophet of very high spiritual insight had spoken of a suffering servant whose sufferings would have vicarious value for mankind. Jesus made himself a Messiah not of a military or spectacular kind, but of the kind envisioned by that ancient prophet. Jesus' death revealed at once the eternal character of God: holy and righteous and incapable of allowing the framework of right-eousness to be violated with impunity, yet infinitely merciful, taking the initiative in the restoration of man to a redeemed status, suffering in order to set right and lift to a new level the whole network of man's relationship to himself. At the Last Supper with his disciples, Jesus broke bread with them and passed to them a cup saying, "This is my body which is broken for you. . . . This cup is the new covenant in my blood." That is how he regarded the death he was about to die.

III

THE BIBLE

17. *Did the Biblical History Truly Take Place?*

A GREAT DEAL of the Bible is occupied with telling us things that are supposed to have taken place during past centuries. The writers of the Bible seemed to feel that it was chiefly through these events that God became known to man. In other words, the religion of the Bible is essentially a historical religion. Therefore, it is quite important to inquire whether the events that are narrated in the Bible really transpired or not.

To get a thoroughgoing answer to this question, it is of course necessary to work through the entire Bible and deal with every portion and every narrative individually and separately. Although this cannot be done here, we can at least give some indication of the general result of such study. If we begin our investigation with the patriarchal narratives,

that is, those concerning Abraham, Isaac, and
Jacob, the forefathers of the Israelite people, we
find that these stories, although they must have
been handed down orally for centuries, fit in very
well with what is now becoming known through
archeological research of ancient life, laws, and
customs in upper Mesopotamia. If we consider the
Exodus, we find that it is possible to identify some
of the sites in Egypt and in the peninsula of Sinai
where the children of Israel are said to have been.
Also, we find that Moses, the founder of Israelite
monotheism, lived not far from the time of a great
Egyptian king who also formulated a monotheistic
belief. The general setting is such that the emergence at that time of the children of Israel into a
more unified people devoted to the worship of the
Lord is thoroughly credible.

If we follow the children of Israel in the conquest of the Promised Land, we find through actual archeological excavation in Palestine that many
Canaanite cities suffered destruction at just about
the time the Israelites are supposed to have come.
Also, at about this time, we find the Israelites
mentioned on an Egyptian monument as a people
actually in Palestine. When we advance to the

time of Solomon, we are able to point to an excavated city in Palestine which was probably one of his chariot cities, and to a seaport city at the head of the Gulf of Aqaba where the same king conducted extensive manufacturing and commercial activities. In the case of yet later kings, we find their actual names appearing on contemporary Assyrian and Babylonian monuments.

As for New Testament times, it is possible in Palestine to identify many of the sites and ways connected with the life of Christ. Also, out in the Mediterranean world, not a few similar identifications are possible with respect to the travels of Paul. For a single example, in telling of Paul's work at Thessalonica, Acts 17:6 calls the city authorities at that place "politarchs." This word is otherwise unknown in all Greek literature, but the very word was actually found in an inscription on a Roman arch still standing in modern times at that city.

By putting together a great many such observations, we arrive at the general conclusion that certainly in its broad outlines, and many times even in its small details, the biblical history truly took place.

18. Does the Bible Agree with Modern Science?

Some people who have accepted science whole-heartedly have, as an apparently necessary conse-quence, attacked the Bible vigorously for its lack of agreement with modern scientific conceptions. On the other hand, there are some valiant defend-ers of the Bible who with equal vigor maintain that the ideas and achievements of modern science are already foreshadowed in the Bible. To give a single example of the latter mode of thought, we may notice an interpretation of Nahum 2:4. This passage reads as follows: "The chariots rage in the streets, they rush to and fro through the squares; they gleam like torches, they dart like lightning." What the prophet Nahum actually was referring to was the battle in which the great city of Nineveh was destroyed in 612 B.C. The kind of interpreta-tion with which we are now dealing, however, supposes that he was looking into the twentieth century A.D. and giving a precise description of modern automobiles! Do they not run like light-

ning, do they not have headlights like torches,
above all, do they not constantly rage in the streets
and rush through the squares?

In a real sense this question so raised is irrel-
evant, for the Bible is not primarily concerned
with the kind of problems to which science devotes
most of its attention. The Bible is concerned with
God's mighty acts and the response of men to
them. In connection with the worship of God, the
Bible refers to the overwhelming impression of
majesty and awesomeness made by the starry heav-
ens. It is concerned with the religious implications
of this fact, not with the computation of the dis-
tance to a given star. Both these matters are proper
objects of concern. The two modes of thought, the
two ways of outreach of the human mind and
spirit, are not in antagonism to each other; rather,
they are complementary the one to the other. The
Bible, of course, reflects the pre-scientific views of
nature which prevailed at the time it was written.
It is only coincidental that these rarely are surprisingly like our own as, for example, in the first chapter of Genesis where the progression of events in
the Creation runs from the making of the in-
animate universe to the creation of animals and,

last of all, of man. The basic point is clear: the main principle of interpretation must remain a recognition of the historical origins of the biblical documents and of their primary religious purpose. We must frankly discard those non-, pre-scientific myths regarding nature which mark the biblical record without confusing them with actual historical occurrences.

19. Were the Writers of the Bible Inspired?

"All scripture," we are told in II Timothy 3:16, "is inspired by God and profitable for teaching, for reproof, for correction, and for training in righteousness." That is a plain statement of high regard for the Scriptures as truly inspired by God. When II Timothy was written, the documents of the New Testament had not yet been collected or even all written, therefore the reference must have been to the Old Testament Scriptures; nevertheless, as the New Testament writings were similarly brought together into a recognized canon, the text may justly be interpreted as applying in its essential import to the entire Bible.

What does it mean to call the biblical writings inspired? To help answer this question, we may recall a statement in II Peter 1:21. Here in relation to the origin of the Scriptures, it is said, "Men moved by the Holy Spirit spoke from God," or according to the reading of some ancient manuscripts, "Moved by the Holy Spirit, holy men of God spoke." The Bible is inspired, we may take it from this passage, because the men who wrote it were inspired. This must mean that they were men of such character and devotion that the Spirit of God could influence them in their thinking and writing. Further, human spirit must be seen to be guided by divine spirit in the selection of certain texts and not others for inclusion in the Christian canon of Holy Scriptures.

Believing in the inspiration of the Bible does not mean arguing that every syllable of it is a direct and infallible utterance of God. We may freely recognize the full part played by the human agents. They were fallible human beings, necessarily men of their times, and of course limited in various ways. If they reflect scientific views, moral standards, and religious insights characteristic of their time, that is precisely what is to be expected.

Nevertheless, through them a word is being spoken that progressively gains in clearness and power and is really and truly the Word of God.

20. How Was the Life of Christ Recorded?

There is only one place where Jesus is said to have written anything. This is in John 8:6, where it is stated that "Jesus bent down and wrote with his finger on the ground." Whatever words he traced in the sand at that time must have been obliterated by the passing breeze or the trampling feet of men. Otherwise, as far as our information goes, Jesus did not himself write down any records. Since there is also no indication of any stenographer's writing down his words as they were uttered, we must assume that at first the sayings of Jesus and the memory of his actions as well were simply preserved in the minds of his hearers and those who associated with him. That there was such a period of oral transmission is not surprising in the least; and, as a matter of fact, it was, comparatively speaking, very brief. In the case of the earlier Old Testament records, some of the materials must have been handed down by word of mouth for hundreds of years. In India, there are important religious texts which were transmitted orally for a thousand years.

The first written records concerning Christ were probably collections of his sayings. We do not have any ancient examples, but we have a striking sample from the third century A.D. This is a sheet of papyrus which was found at the Egyptian town of Oxyrhynchus. The papyrus contains a series of sayings, each introduced with the words, "Jesus says." Some of the sayings are ones which are also to be found in the canonical Gospels; but others would be totally unknown to us save for their fortunate preservation upon this long-buried fragment of papyrus. It seems reasonable to suppose that other collections of the sayings of Jesus had been made at early dates. As a matter of fact, one such extended collection of sayings was, we now think, the earliest written record about the life of Christ. This collection was used as a major source in the compilation of the first and third Gospels, those bearing the names of Matthew and of Luke. There is a strong possibility that the collection of sayings was originally made by the apostle Matthew, and

that it is for this reason that his name is attached
to the Gospel in which these sayings were later in-
corporated. Since the collection was a very important source, German scholars often referred to it by
their corresponding word, *Quelle*. From this, we
derive the customary designation of this hypothet-
ical source as "Q."

The next thing that happened after the com-
position of "Q," as far as we are able to trace the
course of events, was the writing of the Gospel
according to Mark. Early church tradition ascribes
this work to Mark, the companion of Paul and
Peter, and leads us to believe that it was written
at Rome, shortly after Peter lost his life there in
the Neronian persecution. This would seem to be
a very natural situation. When the great apostle
was gone and other eyewitnesses of the life of Jesus
had also died or were growing old, it became very
necessary to commit the record of the life of Christ
to writing. On the whole, Mark's Gospel may be
characterized as a swift account of the things which
Jesus did.

The next step was then, logically enough, the
combining of the account of the doings of Christ
with the collection of his sayings. This was essen-

tially what was accomplished in the Gospels according to Matthew and to Luke. The third Gospel is believed to have been written by Luke, who was "the beloved physician" and the companion of Paul. In the preface to this Gospel, Luke tells how by that time many narratives of the life of Christ had been compiled and how he had traced all things closely and endeavored to write an orderly account of the life of Christ. In Matthew and Luke, the main sources are Mark and "Q," while many other materials have been gathered from yet other sources.

To these three written Gospels, a fourth was later added, the Gospel according to John. It is in the nature of a profound and penetrating meditation upon the innermost significance of the life of Christ. All these Gospels were written in the first century A.D., and in the second century, the writer Irenaeus was able to declare that even as there are four regions of the world and four principal winds, so too the Church, which is scattered over the whole earth, has four strong foundation pillars, namely the four Gospels.

21. Why Did Paul Write Letters?

The letters of Paul were probably written before any of the four Gospels which we have just mentioned. Thus, Paul's letters are the earliest written parts of the New Testament which we now have. It is, therefore, very interesting to ask why it was that Paul came to write these letters.

As we remember, Paul journeyed widely across the Mediterranean world. He believed that Christianity was for everybody, not just for the Jewish people among whom Jesus had lived. The only requirement for a Christian, he taught, is faith, which is an attitude of loving trust in God, through Jesus Christ. Therefore, Paul went constantly to new places to tell new people this universal message. As he went, sometimes he wanted to write ahead to prepare for his coming, and more often, matters came up after he had left a place, which required his attention and called for a communication. In other words, he wrote his letters on all kinds of occasions, naturally connected with the carrying out of his work.

To make this general statement more specific, we may give a few concrete examples. Paul preached the gospel at Thessalonica and afterward sent his associate, Timothy, back to see how matters were, there. He, himself, meanwhile, was at Athens and Corinth. When Timothy returned Paul wrote two letters to express his joy at the good news which Timothy brought and also to give advice on certain problems which Timothy reported had arisen in the church at Thessalonica. These problems included the death of some of the church members, and also the abandonment of work by others who believed that the end of the world would take place any moment.

Not long after this, Paul received word of what had happened over in the Roman province of Galatia in Asia Minor. There he had preached his universal gospel of faith, but afterward certain "Judaizers" had come in and said that it was necessary for any pagan to become a Jew first before he could be a Christian. Paul immediately wrote a vehement letter to declare that Abraham himself had been characterized by faith and that, therefore, anyone who had faith was a spiritual descendant of his and an heir of the promises which God had made to him. Therefore, anyone could be a Christian directly by faith.

Later Paul wrote a series of letters to the church at Corinth where many problems had arisen, including sectarian division, pagan life, attacks on Paul himself, and perplexities about spiritual gifts and the resurrection. Again. Paul wrote a lengthy letter to Rome to prepare for his own visit to the Christian church in that capital of the world.

Paul went to Rome at last, but, sadly enough, as a prisoner. Even so, he could continue writing letters and he did so to churches which had sent him help and which had problems of various kinds.

Paul wrote letters to individuals as well as to churches, and among these perhaps the most striking is a short one-page note to the master of a runaway slave. Paul had converted the runaway slave to Christianity and was sending him back to the master, himself a Christian. In this short letter, he asked the master to receive the runaway back again, "no longer as a slave but more than a slave, as a beloved brother."

Such were the kinds of situations in which Paul penned his letters. All together he wrote more than a dozen which were eventually gathered from the

places to which he had sent them and made into
a collection and an important part of our New
Testament.

22. How Do We Know That We Are Reading What the Original Writers Wrote?

When we read the Bible, how do we know that
we are reading what the original writers of the
documents wrote? The answer to this question involves telling something about the branch of study
which is known as textual criticism. The work in
this field of research includes the discovery of ancient manuscripts and the careful comparison of all
such manuscripts that are known anywhere, in
order to find which are the oldest manuscripts and
what is the true text, as far as it can be recovered,
of the Bible.

Illustrating the story with particular reference to
the New Testament, we may begin by reporting
that the oldest fragment of a New Testament
manuscript now known is a bit of papyrus contain-
ing a few words of the Gospel according to John
from a copy which was made in the first half of

the second century A.D. After that, the next oldest
important manuscript is a copy of the collection of
Paul's letters, also written on papyrus and dating
from around A.D. 200. Then from around A.D. 350,
we have the great parchment manuscripts, the
Vaticanus, kept in the Vatican library at Rome,
and the Sinaiticus, found at Mount Sinai and now
kept in the British Museum at London. After that
there is an ever-increasing number of manuscripts
as we come down across the centuries. All together,
there are over two thousand five hundred manuscripts which bear witness to the text of the New
Testament.

The comparison of these manuscripts with each
other is a very painstaking task. By this labor, it is
possible to group the manuscripts into several great
families and to determine at least approximately
which are the oldest ones. The various manuscripts
do not always exactly agree in their wording, both
because scribes often made mistakes in copying and
also because intentional changes were sometimes
made. It is necessary, therefore, to study every word
in the text and to see how it reads in the various
manuscripts, particularly in the oldest ones. Thus
it is often possible to detect and correct mistakes

and changes which have been made. Of course, every time a new manuscript is discovered, it has to be compared with the ones already known to see if it brings us any additional information. By this long process of scientific work, it is possible to establish the original text of the New Testament with, in most cases, a very high degree of accuracy.

It is because this work is constantly going on and because some of the oldest manuscripts have been discovered in recent years, that it has been necessary to make new translations of the Bible from time to time. The newest translations, based upon the most ancient manuscripts, are extremely accurate.

23.   What Is the Best Translation of the Bible?

The preceding discussion has shown the necessity of making new translations of the Bible from time to time. In general, the translations which have been made may be grouped into two classes. The first class includes the translations made by large bodies of scholars who had some more or less official authorization to undertake the task. Of the English translations produced by such groups of scholars, the most famous is the Authorized, or "King James" Version which was published and dedicated to King James in A.D. 1611. Written in simple, stately, beautiful, and vigorous language, the words of this translation have entered deeply into common speech and general literature. In the judgment of such a distinguished representative of literary pursuits as Mary Ellen Chase, who has devoted one of her books to *The Bible and the Common Reader*,[1] it is the King James Version which is best suited to the uses of the ordinary reader.

With the availability of new manuscripts in the nineteenth century, particularly including Codex Vaticanus which was only then made accessible to outside scholars, and Codex Sinaiticus which was only then discovered in its remote monastery, the necessity for a scholarly revision seemed evident. Such a Revised Version was published in England in 1881 and in America in 1901. Again, in the twentieth century a new revision has been produced. Using yet later discoveries and more accurate still, this is the Revised Standard Version, from which the Bible quotations in this book are taken.

The second general category of translations comprises those made independently by individual scholars or small groups of scholars. Among the most notable of these are the *New Translation* by James Moffatt and the *American Translation* by J. M. Powis Smith, Edgar J. Goodspeed, and others. In general, such translations as these are not only very accurate, but also extremely modern in phrase-ology. Sometimes, too, they make rearrangements in the text in accordance with recent scholarly theories.

All the translations mentioned and others, too, have their great values. Which is "best" to use depends to a considerable extent upon the particular purpose we have in mind at the time. All are valuable aids to our study of the Word of God.

24. What Is the Biblical View of Human Destiny?

The biblical view of human origins is found in the book of Genesis. Man was created by God as a being with a spiritual nature, capable of fellowship and co-operation with his Creator.

The biblical view of human history is found in

the Prophets. Man, both individually and collec-
tively, rebels against the purpose of God and
thereby brings disaster upon himself and his society. In the light of the righteousness of God, and
under the circumstances of man's sinfulness, this
is an inevitable result. The prophets sometimes
used the figure of a plumb line, to suggest that
even as a wall that is found to be crooked cannot
stand but will eventually collapse under the ceaseless pull of the force of gravity, so, too, a nation
whose life is not right will fall. The nature of God
is also that of love, however, and therefore the
prophets declared with equal assurance that if only
a man or nation would repent, a way of restoration
would be opened.

The biblical view of human destiny suggested
already in the hope of the prophets, is worked out
in the New Testament. It is that there will be at
last a kingdom of heaven in which the will of God
will be done perfectly. This kingdom is expected
to come "on earth," yet since "the things that are
seen are transient" its final place must be in an
eternal world which is now unseen.

Is it the ultimate destiny of all mankind to attain
to this kingdom? The answer to this question no

man can know. The book of Revelation pictures the symbolic number of 144,000 persons singing praises to God on the shore of the sea that is like glass mingled with fire, while torment and woe are poured out upon the ungodly. The 144,000 are the martyrs in the persecution of Domitian; the others are the worshipers of the Beast. Surely there must be a difference like that in the destinies of the good and the evil.

Nevertheless, the apostle Paul seems to look forward to an ultimate outcome of God's purposes in an all-comprehending redemption. He views all human history as symbolized in the two epochal figures of Adam and of Christ. The former he equates with sin and death, the latter with obedience and life. Then he declares, "For as in Adam *all* die, so also in Christ shall *all* be made alive" (I Corinthians 15:22). Again, in Romans 11:32, Paul declares, "God has consigned *all* men to disobedience, that he may have mercy upon *all*." In *The Bible Today,*[2] Professor C. H. Dodd interprets the last passage to mean that "as every human being lies under God's judgment, so every human being is ultimately destined, in his mercy, to eternal life." Similarly in Ephesians 1:10 and Colossians 1:20 it is declared to be God's purpose to "unite all things" or "reconcile all things" in Christ. The last goal is "that God may be everything to every one" (I Corinthians 15:28). "This," says Professor Dodd, speaking of the biblical view, "is the final meaning of the entire process in time."

IV

THE CHURCH

25. *When Did the Church Originate?*

THE WORD "church" is the English translation of
the word *ecclesia,* from which root we get such a
word as "ecclesiastical." *Ecclesia* meant fundamen-
tally an assembly, and in relation to Christianity
denoted a gathering or a company of Christians. It
could be used either for a single group of Christians
in one locality or for the whole body of Christians
everywhere.

Upon asking when the church originated, we
come upon two somewhat surprising facts. The
first is, that in the Gospels the word church hardly
ever appears. Its only occurrences are in Matthew
16:18 and 18:17. This is apparently conclusive
proof that Jesus said little or nothing about any
formal organization of his disciples. The second
fact is that in the letters of Paul, the first of which
were written within twenty years after the cruci-

fixion of Christ, there is constant mention of the
church and it is clearly an organization of much
importance and vitality. Two conclusions may be
drawn from the two facts just observed. The first
conclusion is that during the lifetime of Jesus what
later became the church was growing up only
silently and naturally as an informal fellowship.
The second, that whereas the death of the Leader
might have been expected to destroy this incipient
association, on the contrary something happened
very soon thereafter to make it stronger than ever.
According to the traditions of the church itself,
what happened was the resurrection of Christ on the
first day of the week after his death and the special
realization of the influence of his spirit which came
to the disciples sometime after that on the day of
Pentecost.

If the foregoing description of the historical circumstances is correct, then we would not expect to
find that Jesus had laid down any detailed blue-
prints for the organized life of his followers, nor
would we expect that when the church first came
clearly into view it would be other than a spon-
taneous growing thing. Actually this is exactly the
situation which is reflected in the documents of the

New Testament. In the Gospels, we see the disciples eating, journeying, working with Christ. In the letters of Paul, particularly the earlier ones, we see the Christians with a variety of officers and leaders, finding their way gradually toward the most effective form of Christian community. Only in the later writings are the outlines of organization coalescing into quite definite forms. We would say, then, as we look at the whole picture, that the church is not artificial but natural, and that it came into being not as something arbitrarily imposed upon men but as something spontaneously growing up out of the tremendous impact of the life of Christ in the history of the world.

26.   What Is the Roman Catholic Church?

The Roman Catholic Church is the form which Christianity assumed as time went along, particularly in so far as it was centered around Rome. Already in the first century A.D., the growing Christian movement faced many problems. There was a tendency for the Christians to divide into sects, as we saw in connection with Paul's correspondence with the Corinthians. There were also problems of philosophy and of varying teachings on religious subjects, as we may clearly learn from such a letter as that which Paul wrote to the Colossians. In the second century A.D., all these problems continued to exist and even grow more acute. In order to help meet them, the Christian community took three steps which were scarcely on the horizon in the first century.

The first effort was the bringing together of the most important Christian writings that had by then been composed into a canon of officially recognized Scripture. This canon was not defined with absolute finality for another century or two, but the main outlines of it emerged clearly in the second century. In its essential structure, it comprised the four Gospels and the letters of Paul and other "apostles," these two main parts being connected by the book of Acts. Most of these documents were written originally, no doubt, without any anticipation that they would ever be embodied in such an official collection. Nevertheless, the grouping together of all these documents and their acceptance as authoritative, provided materials of extreme importance for the guidance of the growing church.

The second development was the formulation of a symbol, or Rule of Faith, which was in time to become the Apostles' Creed, a short paragraph of condensed Christian belief, which could be used as a test and standard of what it really was to be a Christian. The central ideas of this creed are of course derived from the first century Christian writings, but those writings, themselves, had not contained such a creed in any formalized way.

The third step was the acceptance of the authority of a single bishop in each city. In the twelfth chapter of I Corinthians, we read about a variety of workers in the church, including apostles, prophets, teachers, workers of miracles, healers, helpers, administrators, and speakers in various kinds of tongues. In the letters to Timothy and Titus we hear about bishops, elders, and deacons. The nature of the references is such that we can hardly tell whether the bishop and the elder are at this time one and the same functionary, or different. As the second century advanced, however, the bishop was more and more exalted and the authority of a single bishop in a single city was more and more recognized. To have the right to such authority, the bishop was supposed to have received his commission in a direct line of descent from the apostles.

The emergence of these three developments, the New Testament Canon, the Rule of Faith, and the Apostolic Episcopate (*episcopos* being the Greek word for bishop), is generally recognized as marking the outlines of the emerging Roman Catholic Church. It marked the strengthening of church order and church discipline. But where does the Roman part come in? The answer lies in the fact that the city of Rome was then the capital of the world. Naturally, therefore, the bishop in that city tended to exert a corresponding authority over all Christians everywhere. This authority was heightened by the fact that the two great apostles, Peter and Paul, had both worked and died in Rome. Indeed, the church at Rome believed it possible to trace the commission of its head back through an unbroken succession to Peter himself. This head of the Roman church, who, by virtue of the city in which he presided and of the commission which he was said to have from Peter, claimed authority over all Christians everywhere, eventually became known as the Pope.

27.   What Is the Eastern Orthodox Church?

The Roman ideal was a church that was "always and everywhere the same." Christians did not everywhere and always agree to the leadership of Rome, however. Other cities in addition to Rome had ancient Christian communities and honorable Christian leaders. Besides Rome, the other most important cities were doubtless Constantinople, Alexandria, Antioch, and Jerusalem. While Rome dominated the West, these other four cities tended to form a group in the East. As a matter of fact, each of these cities was the center of a patriarchate or extended ecclesiastical region under the jurisdiction of a bishop who was called a patriarch. From this point of view the patriarchates of Constantinople, Alexandria, Antioch, and Jerusalem formed the Eastern Church, as opposed to the Western Church which comprised the patriarchate of Rome.

The actual division between the East and the West was something that came about only gradually. Contributing forces were political rivalries, linguistic differences, the East speaking Greek and

the West Latin, and temperamental differences, the
East being interested in philosophy and the West
being prevailingly practical. The consummation of
a long drift apart came in the so-called Great Schism
in A.D. 1054. At that time, the Roman Pope, Leo IX,
and the patriarch of Constantinople, Michael
Cerularius, came into controversy. On July 15,
1054, the legates of Leo placed a decree in the
great church of Hagia Sophia which excommuni-
cated Cerularius and all his adherents and called
down upon him condemnation "along with all here-
tics, together with the devil and his angels." The
division between East and West which was made
irrevocable by that action has continued until today.
By the Eastern Orthodox Church is meant not only
the patriarchates already mentioned, but also other
churches founded in the East, for example in the
Balkans and in Russia, which likewise are not in
communion with Rome.

28. What Is Protestantism?

Protestantism is a movement which arose in the
West, and which resulted in a major breaking away

from the Roman Catholic Church. This movement was inaugurated by Martin Luther, himself a Roman Catholic monk in Germany. In the course of profound spiritual struggles, he devoted himself to the study of the New Testament, particularly Paul's letter to the Romans. Finding there the words, "the just shall live by faith," Luther was greatly helped. He began to see that a Christian can go directly to God by faith without the necessity for the mediation of an elaborate ecclesiastical organization. At the same time he became increasingly aware of various abuses within the ecclesiastical machine of which he was a part. The most glaring of these was the peddling of "indulgences." Although the theological definition of it was more refined, an indulgence appeared to the ordinary Christian to be a pardon for his sin and a remission of its penalties purchasable for a certain fee. When a vendor of such indulgences was coming to his city of Wittenberg, Luther challenged the practice in a series of ninety-five theses, which he posted on the door of the castle church and declared himself ready to defend. This event took place in A.D. 1517.

From then on, the controversy developed rapidly and a large number of people rallied to the support of the stand which was being taken by the young monk. Originally, Luther had no thought save that of the correction of certain abuses within the Roman Catholic Church. Ultimately he found himself the leader of a movement which broke away entirely and assumed its own proportions. Among the ideas characteristic of the new movement were those which grew naturally out of the very experience of Martin Luther. These included the reading of the Bible by every man for himself, and the acceptance of the doctrine of justification by faith, whereby every individual Christian had the dignity and the liberty of a direct relationship to God through Christ.

These ideas and others related to them proved immensely effective in the minds of men. They spread rapidly and soon there were other leaders in other lands, promulgating similar and related teachings. These leaders included Zwingli and Calvin in Switzerland, John Knox in Scotland, John Wesley in England, and many others in many other places. It was as a result of all these movements, dedicated to freedom and to faith, that Protestantism arose.

29. Why Are There So Many Different Churches?

In the foregoing sections we have seen how the three major divisions of Christendom came into existence, namely Roman Catholicism, Eastern Orthodoxy, and Protestantism. The Roman Catholic Church has substantially maintained its unity and exists as one centralized ecclesiastical organization, but there are many separate churches within Eastern Orthodoxy and an almost endless number and variety of bodies within Protestantism. Why are there so many different churches? Let us take up this important problem where it is most acute, namely within Protestantism itself.

An essential principle of Protestantism is, as we have seen, that each man should read the Bible for himself and go for himself directly to God through faith in Christ. If each man may read, study, and interpret the Bible for himself there is nothing to keep him, as he does so, from thinking his own thoughts and arriving at his own conclusions. This is exactly what Protestants have done. Set free from the restraining influence of a centralized authority, and inspired by the joy of free perusal of God's word, each group has gone in its own direction.

This is obviously a great and good thing. It means that, unhampered by exterior compulsion, men are following the dictates of their own intellect and conscience in the things of religion. Such liberty is the very genius of Protestantism.

On the other hand, certain of the consequences of this attitude have been lamentable. According to the *Yearbook of American Churches* for 1957, there were at the latest report 258 religious bodies in the United States of America. The Roman Catholic Church was shown as one, the Jewish congregations were counted as one body, and it was the Protestants who accounted for almost all the rest of these numerous groups. Surely it is carrying the principle of Protestantism too far when it results in such an excessive fragmentation. Or perhaps the situation results from the overemphasis upon one principle to the neglect of another. The principle of freedom is certainly implicit in Protestantism and precious to it. But there is another principle in Christianity which should also be cherished and practiced by

Protestantism, namely the principle of fellowship.
Fellowship is just as biblical as freedom. If we study
the Bible and derive from it the great teaching of
faith which enables each of us to stand up in freedom and dignity before God, we need also to pay
heed to the other teaching which was also set forth
by the apostle Paul when he appealed to the divided
Corinthians, "that all of you agree that there be
no dissensions among you, but that you be united
in the same mind and the same judgment."

30. *What Are the Distinctive Emphases of Some of the Churches?*

As each body of Christians has followed the lead-
ing of that portion of the light which has come to
it out of God's word, it has developed certain distinctive emphases. Let us try to describe some of
these.

When one enters a Roman Catholic Church, one
is impressed by a sense of historical continuity.
Napoleon assembled his men for the Battle of the
Pyramids and told them, "Forty centuries of history
look down on you." In a Roman Catholic Church,

nearly twenty centuries of Christian history seem
to look down on us. The language used is still that
of antiquity, the prayers offered by the priests express the same thoughts which are represented in
the paintings of the catacombs beneath Rome.

The Eastern Orthodox Church is distinguished
by its mysticism. This may be vividly realized from
the great church of Hagia Sophia at Constantinople. Here the very architecture is such as to give
a sense of the brooding presence of the Spirit of
God and of the ineffable beauty and peace of that
presence.

The Lutheran Church is marked by faith, such
as Martin Luther himself taught so strongly. In her
book, *Until That Day*,[1] Kressmann Taylor told how
in the days of Hitler the members of a Lutheran
congregation in Berlin assembled only to find their
church roped off and entrance barred by Storm
Troopers. They waited a long time, hoping to be
able to worship. At last they began to move away.
As they did so, someone started Martin Luther's
hymn, *Ein' feste Burg*. All the voices took it up
and they marched away, down the radiating streets,
giving expression to an undefeatable faith in the
words:

A mighty fortress is our God,
A bulwark never failing,
Our helper he, amid the flood
Of mortal ills prevailing.

. . .

And though this world, with devils filled,
Should threaten to undo us,
We will not fear, for God hath willed
His truth to triumph through us.

The Episcopal Church has placed a distinctive emphasis upon the oneness of the Creator-God and the Redeemer-God, and the consequent goodness of his creation. This in turn has led to a distinctive emphasis upon beauty. Concerning one of its great cathedrals, Dr. Ralph Adams Cram spoke as chief architect, "This building will stand for a minimum of 2,000 years and will minister to 20,000,000 people in that time. Suppose it does cost $30,000,000? A superdreadnaught costs as much, serves a destructive end, and at the end of twenty-five years has to be scrapped." Such is the importance attached to the making of a beautiful place for the worship of God in the traditions of this church.

The Presbyterian Church has been marked by

its devotion to the exposition of the Bible. Its ministers have excelled in expository preaching, and as they have explained a single word of sacred writ, it has become luminous and vitally effective. The Methodist Church has been characterized by the spirit of the Crusade. Charles and John Wesley preached and sang their warmhearted message throughout England, and soon thereafter Robert Raikes began to gather children into Sunday Schools, John Howard took up the struggle for prison reform, and Wilberforce began his battle against slavery. The Congregational Church has stood for freedom, and it was from its circles that the Pilgrim Fathers came to America. The Baptist Church has staunchly advocated the separation of church and state, and has risen to the defense of this great principle at every crisis. The Disciples of Christ have pleaded for unity in the midst of a divided Christendom. The Society of Friends has explored the silences and derived strength and insight from waiting quietly for the light to shine within the human soul.

Such are some of the distinctive emphases of some of the churches. Certainly no single church has a monopoly on any single emphasis which we have mentioned. Yet each has made the one mentioned a specially characteristic mark of its common life. As we survey them all, these various emphases would seem to be not contradictory but complementary aspects of the total life of Christendom.

31. What Attitude Should I Take Toward People of Other Beliefs?

As we look at the whole multifarious and variegated picture of the existing Christian world, we sometimes see aspects of it which strike us as strange. Some names seem queer and some practices peculiar. In such a situation, it is helpful to remember the words, "No great soul ever laughed at anything that was sacred to another soul." Instead of reacting with scorn toward that which is unfamiliar to ourselves, it seems desirable to strive for sympathetic understanding. As a matter of fact, what we ourselves believe may appear queer to someone else! Therefore, it behooves us all to be considerate of one another's beliefs.

This does not, of course, mean that one will never make any choices as to what he himself wishes to believe. The total variety of belief and practice is so great that one person can hardly comprehend it all in his own mind and behavior. He is necessarily driven to select that formulation of faith and that method of expression which seem to him most nearly in accord with the truth and in harmony with his own needs and aspirations. Thus, it may well be that there will continue to be varieties of faith and practice in line with varying understanding and need; but among all these religious groups let us have the grace of mutual appreciation.

32. Will the Churches Ever Unite?

One of the most encouraging signs in the whole Christian movement today is the strong tendency toward unity. This manifests itself in the first place in a strong sense of sorrow for the many divisions of Christianity. A classic expression of this feeling was given in the following words at a modern world conference of churches: "We humbly acknowledge that our divisions are contrary to the will of Christ and we pray God in his mercy to shorten the days of our separation and to guide us by his spirit into fullness of unity."

A second mark of this tendency is a renewed emphasis upon the things in which the churches are already united. It is easy enough to put the emphasis upon the things by which we are separated. Instead of looking for these things, arguing about them, and magnifying them, there is a strong interest now in discovering, holding up, and making important the things on which all Christians already are agreed. There are surprisingly many of these things, and a genuine spiritual unity already exists among a great host of Christians who are superficially divided into separate bodies. Indeed, if it were not for the existence and steady growth of this underlying spiritual unity, it would be futile to talk about or strive for outward organizational unity.

A third mark of what is happening is the strengthening of co-operative movements among the churches. There are many kinds of these oriented toward various specific purposes. Some of these movements simply call themselves "Christian," without reference to denominationalism, and proceed with urgent tasks which lie before them. Thus, for example, we have the Young Men's Christian Association and the Young Women's Christian Association devoted to work with young men and women in the inclusive spirit of Christianity. Again we have organizations which make explicit recognition of the major divisions among religious bodies, all having their common background in the Bible, and endeavor to promote tolerance by the building of mutual understanding. Here one thinks, for example, of the National Conference of Christians and Jews.

Again there are councils of churches, organized on a community, state, national, or world basis. The bodies which are united in these organizations retain their autonomy, but co-operate voluntarily in common tasks. Speaking nationally, we have the National Council of the Churches of Christ in America; and looking to the world, we have the World Council of Churches.

There is yet another level at which the achievement of Christian unity is progressing. This is the level of nothing less than organic union. Already some notable mergers of what were formerly separate denominations have taken place. Such unions have been accomplished not only in the United States but also in other lands. In South India, for example, a plan has been put into effect through which denominations with widely variant patterns of thought and organization have actually become one church.

Hitherto, to be entirely honest, we perhaps should have sung "Onward, Christian Soldiers" with those words proposed by William H. Hudnut, Jr., in a 1944 copy of *The Christian Century*:

> Like a halting caravan
> > Moves the Church of Christ;
> We are feebly faltering
> > Toward our timid tryst.
> We are all divided,
> > Many bodies we,
> Kept apart by doctrine
> > And lack of charity.

As a result of the many movements now in progress, some of which we have just described, the original words of the hymn are becoming more and more truly applicable:

> Like a mighty army
> > Moves the Church of God;
> Brothers we are treading
> > Where the saints have trod;
> We are not divided,
> > All one body we,
> One in hope and doctrine,
> > One in charity.

V

IMMORTALITY

33. *Do You Believe in the Soul?*

THE IDEA of the soul is very old. It is thought by some investigators that the idea originated in the experience of dreams. We may picture a primitive man lying in his cave asleep. During the night he dreams that he is in a distant place hunting wild animals. Next morning he awakes in his same place in the cave and, remembering the dream, can only conclude that his soul journeyed afar during the night. There are other experiences which may have contributed to the rise of the same idea. The observation of the shadow which so mysteriously comes and goes with a man is thought by some to have played a part in this. It may be more likely that when primitive man saw the blood flow from a wounded enemy or noted that the breath was gone out of a deceased man, he concluded that this was the substance of life and the residence of the soul. At all events, the conception was clearly in existence from very early times that a man was not only a physical body but also some kind of relatively immaterial essence.

The idea of the breath was influential in the selection of the actual words which were employed to designate this immaterial essence in the make-up of a man. As far as the Bible is concerned, "soul" and "spirit" are the two terms most frequently found. The word for soul is *nephesh* in the Hebrew language and *psyche* in the Greek. Both mean primarily "breath," and *nephesh* is so translated, for example, in Job 41:21. In other cases the same word may be rendered "living being," "life," "person," or "self." Perhaps "self" comes as near as any English word can to being a comprehensive rendering. The Hebrew word usually translated spirit is *ruah,* and the corresponding Greek term is *pneuma.* Again, both these words have as their basic meaning "breath" or "wind." For one place to show how these words are used in the Bible we may turn to I Thessalonians 5:23 where Paul prays for the Christians: "May your spirit and soul and body be kept sound and blameless." As Professor Millar Burrows points out in *An Outline of Biblical The-*

ology,[1] the underlying conception of personality found in the Bible seems to be a unity of body animated by the soul (life), and with a higher nature (spirit) which may be possessed by the Spirit of God.

If some such view as the Bible presents should happen not to appear convincing to us what is the alternative? One alternative is that which is frequently chosen in modern thought, namely the conclusion that man is a purely physical being. There is no doubt that man's body can be analyzed into its chemical constituents and that the working of his nervous system can be described in terms of stimulus and reaction. There is considerable doubt, however—indeed, there may be said to be complete confusion—on the matter of how a chemical compound can be aware of itself and of how in a stimulus-reaction cycle there can be any selectivity and free choice. Such things as these and others, however, namely self-consciousness, freedom, awareness of a world of values, and a sense of the infinite, are exactly the distinguishing marks of human personality and therefore constitute the crux of the problem. Having recognized that the highest attributes of human personality are completely inexplicable on the materialistic hypothesis, we are driven to return to the belief in the soul. Man is not only a physical creature, he is also a spiritual being. He possesses qualities which cannot be explained from the material world alone; he is properly described in his inmost being as a soul.

34. Is There Any Empirical Evidence of Survival After Death?

The scientific method of empiricism means the pursuit of truth by observation and experiment. When one asks about the soul and the possibility of its survival after death, it is natural to attempt to gain data on the matter by observation and experiment. There are two areas of investigation which have at least some bearing on the matter. The first is that of parapsychology, in which psychological occurrences of a nature hitherto inexplicable are explored. It is claimed, by investigators like Professor J. B. Rhine, that the mind is at least occasionally able to gain information through other than the normal channels of sense perception. This faculty is now commonly called extrasensory perception and includes both telepathy and clairvoyance. The existence of this power of the mind is attested by a large number of experiments of which the results are difficult to explain fully by chance. The same sort of thing has been observed by a great number of scattered people. For a single impressive example, we may recall that set of events when Sir Hubert Wilkins was flying over the Arctic Ocean and by prearrangement an experimenter in New York City was recording his impressions of what happened. Detailed notations on occurrences, later confirmed when the explorer returned, included awareness of a fire on the ground, of engine trouble in the air, of icing on the wings, and of low circling of the plane over an icy waste correctly identified as to its geographical location. It cannot yet be affirmed that psychologists in general are agreed either upon the actuality of these occurrences or upon their explanation. If data of this sort continue to accumulate and are accepted as conclusive proof that the mind is, upon occasion, capable of functioning without limitation of space and time, it will not necessarily prove the immortality of the self but it will at least point in the direction of that possibility. To the person of modern scientific training, probably the greatest difficulty in the way of belief in immortality is the inability to conceive how the self can exist apart from the physical organism in which it is now at home. If scientific evidence is already available of the ability of the mind to transcend, at least sometimes, the limits of the physical, this is certainly confirmatory of the possibility of survival beyond death. In *The Reach of the Mind*[2] Professor Rhine affirms that extrasensory research has given a "positive suggestion" in favor of such survival.

The second area of investigation has been called spiritualism. Here the effort is made by actual experiment to communicate with or receive communications from the spirits of the deceased. As Frederic W. H. Myers says in the introduction to his *Human Personality and Its Survival of Bodily Death*,[3] "If in truth souls departed call to us, it is to them that we shall listen most of all." Unfortunately, the investigations in this realm have not always been conducted in a truly scientific spirit, and Houdini, for example, after extensive studies declared, "Everything which I have investigated up to the present time has been the result of deluded brains or those which were too actively willing to

believe . . . Nothing I have read concerning the
so-called spiritualistic phenomena has impressed me
as being genuine." The most that can be said at
this time, therefore, is that scientific investigation
is welcome in any field and that if ever authentic
results are attained in this area, they should be
made known to the world in the interest of science.
Among others, Sherwood Eddy believes that such
results have been obtained, and the kind of examples he gives may be studied in his book, *You
Will Survive After Death.*[4]

35. Is the Nature of the Self Such That Im-
mortality Is Probable?

As far as scientific evidence is concerned, at least
some data are beginning to appear which suggest
that there is something about a person which is
capable of functioning beyond the limitations of the
physical body and therefore is potentially capable
of survival beyond death. What is the situation
when the same problem is approached from the
philosophical point of view? Here we come upon
the perfectly familiar yet strangely mysterious fact

of self-transcendence. The self is able to observe itself, judge itself, guide and shape itself. With this
profound fact William Ernest Hocking has dealt in
his book, *Thoughts on Death and Life*.[5] He analyzes
the self as possessing two aspects, one of which he
calls the "excursive" self, and the other the "reflective" self. The excursive self is a personality as it
goes out into the affairs of the world, mingles with
people, has possessions, and attains knowledge. In
these forays into affairs, the excursive self proceeds
from a center, however, and again and again reports
back to the center. There, behind the scenes, the
reflective self is that which initiates these activities,
subjects them to critical examination, and guides
them toward planned goals. The excursive self is
therefore fluctuating, temporal, and limited, but the
reflective self possesses a relative stability, continuity, and transcendence which enable it to play a
creative role. The excursive self comes sooner or
later to an end. It is the self which the world
knows, and which at death is a finished thing, a
life as it is known in the fabric of history. But the
realization that all the while the self within has
been busied with the making of this self without,
raises the strong surmise that in another world it

may go on in its creative activity. Death may therefore mean for the reflective self, Professor Hocking
concludes, not at all the end, but rather "the gong
of passage" from a limited apprenticeship in creative
work to the expanded possibilities of a vaster canvas
and a freer exercise of a more mature art.

36. What Is the Moral Argument for Immortality?

The empirical and philosophical approaches
which we have sketched thus far make immortality
seem possible; the moral argument is that it is not
only possible but that it also ought to be. As shown
by the quotations which we shall shortly give, this
line of reasoning was followed by such eminent
thinkers as Plato and Kant.

The moral argument has two chief aspects. The
first lies in the recognition that justice demands
immortality. In this life there are all kinds of
inequalities and terrible wrongs. The evils of life
do not fall upon those who appear to deserve them
and leave untouched those who are righteous. In
Thornton Wilder's The Bridge of San Luis Rey,[6]

Brother Juniper undertook to make a tabulation on this matter from the point of view that God rewards men in this life according to their just deserts. A pestilence visited Brother Juniper's village and he drew up a diagram of the characteristics of fifteen victims and fifteen survivors, rating them for such items as goodness, piety, and usefulness. When he added up the total for the victims and compared it with the total for the survivors, his figures showed that the dead were five times more worth saving than those who had lived through the pestilence. This unexpected result caused Brother Juniper great distress of mind, and though we ourselves may not go at the matter in the same manner or with the same presuppositions as he, we too cannot escape an overwhelming impression of the terrible inequities of human life.

Is this then the final outcome of things in our universe? Is the outward fortune or misfortune which attends a man in this life the final word? When a ruthless dictator flourishes in his cruelty and a great saint perishes in his dungeon, is that the end of the matter? Is it right that things should come out like that? In the face of such circumstances, the belief in immortality arises as a demand that righteousness shall prevail in the universe, that at long last there shall be some recompense and some reward commensurate with justice, with compassion and with mercy. This side of the matter was set forth by Plato in the following words: "In the case of the just man, we must assume that, whether poverty be his lot, or sickness, or any other reputed evil, all will work for his final advantage, either in this life or in the next. For unquestionably, the gods can never neglect a man who determines to strive earnestly to become just, and by the practice of virtue to grow as much like God as man is permitted to do."

The other aspect of the problem as considered from the moral point of view is this. The moral life constitutes a long endeavor to attain goodness. It is oriented toward ideals, and these ideals have an infinite quality which makes them ever recede from our grasp, ever surpass our reach. Are we then being deceived in our idealism? Or is the universe the kind of place where these ideals do not at last make mock of us? We struggle up the steep slope of moral life and are cut down by death before attaining the summit. Is that the end? Or is there an opportunity beyond death to come closer to those gleaming high peaks which have been glimpsed already in this life? Kant pursues this line of reasoning and arrives at the affirmative conclusion, "The highest good is . . . practically possible, only if we presuppose the immortality of the soul." Such in essential outline are the strong grounds for belief in immortality which are found in a consideration of the moral nature of the universe.

37.   Did Jesus Teach That There Is Life After Death?

In Jesus' time as in our own, there was a division of opinion about life after death. Not a great deal is said about it in the Old Testament until we come to the plaintive question of Job, "If a man die, shall he live again?" and the splendid affirmation of Daniel, "And many of those who sleep in the dust of the earth shall awake. . . . And those who are wise shall shine like the brightness of the firmament; and those who turn many to righteousness, like the stars for ever and ever." Since this explicit doctrine of the resurrection did not appear until rather late in the Old Testament it may be that those who refused to accept it felt that they were the true conservatives who were maintaining the old beliefs.

At any rate we know that in the first century the Sadducees denied the resurrection and the Pharisees believed in it. This question on which there was sharp difference of contemporary opinion was brought to Jesus for an answer. As we are told in the twelfth chapter of the Gospel according to Mark and the parallel passages in Matthew and Luke, the inquiry was made by the Sadducees who naturally presented the matter in the most unfavorable light possible. They cited a case which could actually have happened under Jewish law where a woman had been married to seven brothers, one after another, all of whom had died. The Sadducees, intending to make survival after death appear ridiculous, asked, "In the resurrection whose wife will she be?" Jesus answered by pointing out that they were making a great mistake in supposing that conditions in the next life would simply be a replica of those here. It does not seem necessary to take his words as meaning that there will be no personal relationships whatsoever in the after life since it is in these relationships that some of the highest values known on earth are found. What he does make clear is that the life beyond will not simply be a continuation of the life here with all its perplexities and troubles, but will be something radically and wonderfully different. Then continuing in his reply and using the kind of argument that would be most effective with his questioners, he urged them to go back to the earliest parts of the Scriptures and see what was implied there as to the life after death. "Have you not read in the book of Moses," said Jesus, "how God said to him, 'I am the God of Abraham, and the God of Isaac, and the God of Jacob'? He is not God of the dead, but of the living; you are quite wrong." The statement cited is to be found in Exodus 3:6 and is evidently interpreted by Jesus to mean that the patriarchs of the past live even now in the presence of God. Thus with a kind of answer which was suited to the way in which the question was brought to him, Jesus clearly affirmed that there is life after death. The God whom he made known is not going to preside at the last over a lifeless universe; personality is the most precious thing he has made and it is safe in the keeping of his everlasting purpose.

38. May We Believe in the Resurrection of Jesus Christ?

We cannot help believing in the resurrection, although we cannot entirely explain it. All the Gospels contain some records relating to the resurrection. Paul, also, who wrote before any of our Gospels were composed, placed strong emphasis upon the resurrection. Indeed, he said flatly that if Christ has not been raised from the dead, Christian preaching is in vain and Christain faith is in vain. Beyond the testimony of these honorable men, we have the witness of history itself. We know that the disciples were utterly crushed by the crucifixion of Jesus. When he was taken captive, they left him and fled. After his death they evidently returned to their old occupations. All their hopes had gone for nought. Then, not long after, we find them reassembled, renewed in faith, and restored in courage. Indeed, they have an access of power which they had not had before. Nothing now can stop them. They go across all the world of their day with the message of Jesus Christ.

When we try to explain exactly what happened, we are, to be sure, at a loss. The Gospel records tell many different things. Paul himself speaks as if the resurrection appearances of Christ to his disciples had been of the same kind as the experience which came to himself on the Damascus road. And of that experience, several accounts were current in the early church. Perhaps, at least for the purpose of this brief answer, it is best to content ourselves with recalling the unequivocal assertion of Paul that Christ died for our sins in accordance with the Scriptures, that he was buried, that he was raised on the third day in accordance with the Scriptures, and that he appeared to Cephas, then to the twelve, then to more than five hundred brethren at one time, then to James, then to all the apostles, and last of all, says Paul, "he appeared also to me."

The details of the resurrection and the nature of the spiritual body in which the immortal spirit is clothed are matters which lie beyond human comprehension. But if we are asked whether we believe that the life of Jesus Christ was ended by death and that was all there was to it, or that beyond death he was raised to everlasting spiritual life, that he is a living presence in the world, and that at the

end of the world he will be triumphantly vindicated
in the kingdom of God which he died to establish,
there can be no doubt as to our answer. Such
faith, far from mere credulity, really does not rest
on the foregoing empirical observations. In the
life, death, and resurrection of Jesus, immortality
is seen to be a gracious act of God. We know that
we shall live, not because mortality or the nature of
the self implies it, but ultimately because he lives.

39. *What Effect Has Christianity Had on Belief About Death and Immortality?*

The effect Christianity has had on belief about
death and immortality can be appreciated only if
we know the ideas which prevailed among large
numbers of people in the world into which Christianity came. A great many funeral inscriptions
have now been collected from the ancient Roman
Empire, and they give us a frank glimpse of beliefs
then current. Here are some actual epitaphs recovered by the archeologists: "I paid my debt to
nature and have departed." "I was; I am not; I do
not care." "What I have eaten and what I have

drunk, that is all that belongs to me." "While I lived, I drank willingly; drink, ye who live." "Eat, drink, play, come hither." Such are some typical expressions of the materialism, hedonism, and cynicism which prevailed widely. Behind it, hidden by the flippant words, was an emptiness of life and perhaps not seldom a suppressed but profound sorrow.

That the atmosphere of the New Testament was very different we know well. For a single example, we may recall Paul's word to the Thessalonian Christians, "that you may not grieve as others do who have no hope." That the Christians actually did have an utterly different attitude from the hopeless cynicism of the epitaphs above quoted is made unmistakable by their own funeral inscriptions. Many of these have been preserved in the catacombs at Rome. There we read such words as the following and many others expressive of a like faith: "May his sleep be in peace." "Thou wilt live in God." "Thou wilt live forever." "May God refresh thy spirit." "Mayest thou live in the Lord Jesus." That is the difference which Christianity made!

40. What Will Heaven Be Like?

If the lines of thought which we have been following are valid, then at least certain general conclusions may be drawn as to the nature of life after
death. In the first place, we have maintained that
man has a spiritual nature which is not wholly
explained by chemistry and material facts, and that
this nature has at least a certain kinship with the
fundamental reality in the universe which is likewise spiritual. We may believe, therefore, that after
death the spirit of man will come into closer touch
with the Spirit of God. Since God is best known
to us in Jesus Christ, that will also mean coming
closer to him who is, as we believe, already with
God. Expressions of this truth in the Bible include
Revelation 21:3—"God himself will be with them";
and I John 3:2—"Beloved, we are God's children
now; it does not yet appear what we shall be, but
we know that when he appears we shall be like him,
for we shall see him as he is."

In the second place, we have reasoned that some-
where sometime the books of life must balance out.

All sorrow and suffering must some way be healed. The Bible declares that this, too, will be: "He will wipe away every tear from their eyes, and death shall be no more, neither shall there be mourning nor crying nor pain any more, for the former things have passed away" (Revelation 21:4).

In the third place, we have noted that man strives for infinite ideals and have said that therefore there must be, beyond the frustrations of this life, further opportunity to come closer to those gleaming summits which from here are only glimpsed afar. If this is correct, then the life beyond must be not a thing of monotony and stagnation but of continued progress and achievement. To be sure, rest from labor is a part of our picture of heaven, but perhaps to "lie down for an aeon or two," as Rudyard Kipling put it, will suffice in that regard. And then "the Master of All Good Workmen shall set us to work anew!"

If, beyond these general conclusions toward which our whole discussion seems to tend, we ask for specific and detailed descriptions of the heavenly life, we must confess that this is a matter which lies beyond the bounds of human reason. In seeking for such descriptions, we turn naturally to the

Revelation of John, but even there we find that the
author writes with a remarkable restraint. When he
speaks of heavenly things, he rarely ventures to
say that they *are* thus and so, but only that they
are *like* this or that. He takes the most beautiful
things he knows on earth, the jasper and the
emerald, the rainbow and the sea, and declares that
what he envisions in heaven is "like" these things.
They are the least inadequate comparisons he knows
to employ to suggest something which is ineffably
wonderful. In the same spirit Paul looks forward
to "what no eye has seen, nor ear heard, nor the
heart of man conceived, [namely] what God has
prepared for those who love him."

DOCUMENTATION BY CHAPTERS

I. *God*

1. Chapel Hill, N. C.: University of North Carolina Press, 1932.
2. Psalms 8:3,4, Revised Standard Version of the Holy Bible (New York: Thomas Nelson & Sons, 1953).

II. *Jesus Christ*

1. New York: The Macmillan Company, 1944.
2. New York: Charles Scribner's Sons, 1942.
3. Nashville, Tenn.: Abingdon Press, 1947.
4. London: Hodder & Stoughton, Ltd., 1938.

III. *The Bible*

1. New York: The Macmillan Company, 1952.
2. New York: The Macmillan Company, 1947.

IV. *The Church*

1. New York: Duell, Sloan & Pearce, Inc., 1942.

V. *Immortality*

1. Philadelphia: Westminster Press, 1946.
2. New York: William Sloane Associates, Inc., 1947.
3. New York: Longmans, Green & Co., Inc., 1954.
4. New York: Rinehart & Company, Inc., 1950.
5. New York: Harper & Brothers, 1937.
6. New York: Grosset & Dunlap, Inc., 1944.

SUGGESTED READINGS

I. God

Baillie, John, *The Idea of Revelation in Recent Thought* (New York: Columbia University Press, 1956). The author of an earlier book on *Our Knowledge of God* (New York: Charles Scribner's Sons, 1939) writes here particularly of how God makes himself known.

Hordern, William, *A Layman's Guide to Protestant Theology* (New York: The Macmillan Company, 1955). A very readable introduction to present-day theological thought among Protestant Christians.

II. Jesus Christ

Baillie, Donald M., *God Was in Christ*, 2d ed. (London: Faber and Faber, Ltd., Publishers, 1948). A freshly helpful presentation of the Christian doctrine of the incarnation.

Wilder, Amos N., *New Testament Faith for Today* (New York: Harper & Brothers, 1955). The contemporary relevance of the New Testament proclamation of Jesus Christ.

III. The Bible

Anderson, Bernhard W., *Rediscovering the Bible* (New York: Association Press, 1951). When it is "rediscovered" in this way the Bible has a living message for today.

Richardson, Alan, and Schweitzer, W., eds., *Biblical Authority for Today* (Philadelphia: Westminster Press, 1951). A World Council of Churches symposium on the authority of the Bible particularly with regard to social and political questions.

IV. THE CHURCH

Newbigin, Lesslie, *The Household of God* (New York: Friendship Press, 1954). An ecumenical leader writes about the church in its divisions and its unity.

Spike, Robert W., *In But Not Of the World* (New York: Association Press, 1957). A fresh approach to what the characteristics of the New Testament church can mean in the setting of life today.

V. IMMORTALITY

Baillie, John, *And the Life Everlasting* (New York: Charles Scribner's Sons, 1934). A classic exposition of the Christian faith in eternal life.

Brunner, Emil, *Eternal Hope* (London: Lutterworth Press, 1954). In this book the distinctive Christian hope for eternal life and the kingdom of God stands out against the background of disappointing secular hopes.